The Usborne
Book of
Classroom
Jokes

D1390978

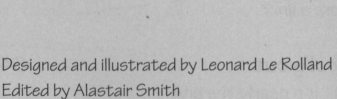

Designed and illustrated by Leonard Le Rolland
Edited by Alastair Smith
Researched by Laura Howell
Managing designer: Ruth Russell

CONTENTS

attention

i must pay more ~~attention~~ in class

i must pay more attention in class

i must pay more attention in class

i must pay more attention in class

i must pay more attention in class

i must pay more attention in class

i must pay more attention in class

i must pay more attention in class

i must pay more attention in class

i must pay more attention in class

i must pay more attention in class

i must pay more attention in class

i must pay more attention in

Class War!

mr. smith

If you add 34,312 and 76,188, divide the total by 3 and multiply it by 4, what do you get?

The wrong answer!

Teacher: Jimmy, which two words, in English, have the most letters?

Jimmy: Post Office.

Teacher: Martina, why did you say that English homework is similar to going to jail for murder?

Martina: Because they both involve long sentences!

What's another name for a collection of bees?

Above average grades.

Teacher: Now, can anyone count to ten in German?

Class: Nein!

Teacher: Hmm, that's not bad for a start.

Teacher: I asked you to draw a cow eating grass. Where's the grass?

Pupil: Well, you were out of the classroom for so long that the cow ate all the grass.

Pupil: Monsieur Gaston, is it true that French teachers only eat one egg for breakfast?

Monsieur Gaston: Yes, for French people, one egg is always *un oeuf*.

Blah blah blah blah blah blah blah blah

What do you call someone who keeps talking when people are no longer interested?

A teacher.

Teacher: Doris, can you name something that is brown and sticky?

Doris: A stick.

Psst. What's white when it's dirty and black when it's clean?

A blackboard.

Teacher: Can anybody tell me which days begin with the letter "T"?

Pupil: Me sir! "Today" and "tomorrow".

Teacher: Joey, what has wheels and flies?

Joey: A refuse truck.

Teacher: Can anybody tell me what happens to something, such as a car, when it rusts?

Pupil: Yeah, someone sells it to my dad, for our family car.

General nonsense

Which month has 28 days?

All of them.

A salary is a form of wages, where the worker is paid a guaranteed amount every month. For example, I am paid a salary. Any questions?

Yes. Where do you work, sir?

Frank, how do you manage to get so many things wrong in a day?

Because I get here so early, sir.

Can anybody tell me, what's a spaceman?

You park your car in it, man!

If you have a referee in soccer, what do you have in bowls?

Soup.

I have 100 eyes, four wings and six legs. What am I?

But miss, you have two eyes, two legs and no wings.

No, no. If I say that I have 100 eyes, four wings and six legs, what would you say that I am?

A liar, miss?

Miss Smith, does money grow on trees?

Of course not.

Then why *do* banks have branches?

Inglish

Joey, R-O-X does not spell rocks.

What does it spell then?

Teacher: Tracey, what's the plural of mouse?

Tracey: Mice.

Teacher: Excellent. Now, what's the plural of baby?

Tracey: Twins!

Teacher: Nicky, spell mouse.

Nicky: M-O-U-S.

Teacher: Not bad. But what's on the end?

Nicky: A tail?

Teacher: If can't is short for cannot, what is "don't" short for?

Pupil: Doughnut?

Teacher: What's the longest sentence you can think of, Frankie?

Frankie: Life imprisonment, Mr. Jones.

Teacher: Clara, I told you to write this out ten times to improve your spelling. You've only done it seven times.

Clara: Sorry, miss. My counting isn't too hot either.

Ali, name two pronouns.

Who? Me?

Teacher: What are you writing, Sarah?

Sarah: A letter to myself, sir.

Teacher: And what does it say?

Sarah: I don't know. I won't receive it till tomorrow.

Johnny, can you give me a sentence with a direct object?

You're beautiful, sir.

Thanks Johnny, but what was the object?

A good report at the end of term.

Teacher: Christopher, what word, if pronounced right, is wrong, but if pronounced wrong, is right?

Christopher: Wrong, Miss Smith.

Teacher: Right!

Teacher: What's the opposite of woe, Joe?

Joe: Giddy up!

Teacher: Today, we'll continue our reading of Shakespeare's Hamlet.

Class: But sir, our class isn't doing Hamlet.

Teacher: Oh. Is this room 2B, or not 2B?

Teacher: Martina, can you give me a sentence beginning with I?

Martina: I is the…

Teacher: No, no, no! You must always say, "I am…"

Martina: I am the ninth letter of the alphabet.

Teacher: Give me a sentence using the word "diploma".

Pupil: My water pipes burst so dad called diploma.

Teacher: Give me a sentence using the word "fascinate".

Pupil: I have a coat with nine buttons, but I can only fascinate.

Teacher: Give me a sentence using the word "information".

Pupil: Geese sometimes fly information.

In the lab

Name a liquid that doesn't freeze.

Hot water!

Teacher: How many planets are there out in space?

Class: All of them.

Teacher: What's the most important lesson you learn in chemistry class, Stan?

Stan: Never lick the spoon!

Teacher: How do you make a science teacher into a mad scientist?

Pupil: Er, step on her toes?

Teacher: How do you prevent diseases caused by biting insects?

Pupil: Don't bite insects, sir.

Teacher: What's the chemical formula for water?

Pupil: H-I-J-K-L-M-N-O.

Teacher: No, of course not!

Pupil: But last week you told us that the chemical formula for water is H_2O.

Teacher: I'm going to give you all a chemistry exercise for your homework.

Class: Cool! Will we be pumping ions?

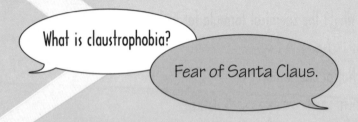

What is claustrophobia?

Fear of Santa Claus.

Teacher: What happened when electricity was first discovered?

Pupil: Somebody got a very bad shock, sir.

Teacher: Carrie, can you name four members of the cat family?

Carrie: A mother cat, a father cat, and two kittens.

What has big ears and a trunk?

A mouse on vacation.

Teacher: If I were to say that I was the planet Neptune, and that this desk is the Sun, and then I started running around the desk, what would you say I was doing?

Pupil: Going crazy, sir?

Teacher: If you pull the wings off a fly, what happens?

Pupil: It becomes a walk.

William, besides wood, can you name a poor conductor?

The music teacher, sir.

Teacher: How can you prove that the Earth is round, Billy?

Billy: Please, sir, I never said that it was.

Teacher: Tell me how we can keep milk from turning sour.

Pupil: Leave it in the cow, sir.

Teacher: Today we'll be learning about electricity.

Class: Cool. Maybe you'll say something shocking.

Geography

Teacher: Why do birds fly south for the winter?

Class: Because it's too far to walk!

Teacher: Rosie, can you name two French wine growing regions.

Rosie: Red and white, sir.

Teacher: Carrie, which country do you like best?

Carrie: Azerbaijan.

Teacher: Can you spell it, please?

Carrie: I've changed my mind. France!

Teacher: What should you do if it rains cats and dogs?

Pupil: Take care not to stand in a poodle.

Teacher: Where are the Andes, Tracey?

Tracey: At the end of your sleevees?

Teacher: Today, I'm going to instruct you on the Alps.

Class: Wow. Will we be back for lunch?

Teacher: Find Australia on the map for me, Fred.

Fred: There it is, Miss Smith.

Teacher: Now, can anyone tell me who discovered Australia?

Another pupil: Fred did.

What is so unusual about Mississippi?

Um... it's got four eyes but it can't see a thing.

Where is the English Channel?

Not sure, Miss Smith. Our TV doesn't receive it.

Name an animal that lives in Lapland.

Reindeer.

Can you name another?

Another reindeer.

Liz, why didn't you do your geography homework?

Well, my dad says that the world is constantly changing, so I thought I'd wait until it's settled down a bit.

Lenny, can you name two small rivers that run into the Nile.

The juve-niles?

Why are you just wearing one glove?

Well, the weather forecast said that today it might be warm, but on the other hand it might be cold.

Why did you say that there are no secrets at the North Pole?

Because at the North Pole your teeth always chatter.

Where can you find an ocean without water?

On a map.

Music to your ears

Why is the music teacher holding a shoe to his ear?

Because today's lesson is about soul music.

Teacher: If "f" means *forte*, what does "ff" stand for?

Pupil: Eighty?

Teacher: Wendy, you've been learning the violin for eight years now, and you still can't hit a note.

Wendy: But you've only just told me that I don't have to blow it!

Teacher: Stan, stop playing that trumpet, you're driving me crazy!

Stan: I think you might be crazy already...
I stopped ten minutes ago.

Pupil: How can I improve my guitar playing, Mr. Lee?

Mr. Lee: Leave it in its case.

Pupil: Hey, sir, what fish do piano menders like most?

Teacher: Tuna, of course!

Pupil: Miss Smith, is a tuba bad for your teeth?

Miss Smith: Not if it's a tuba toothpaste it isn't.

Pupil: Miss, what happens if you drop a piano down a mine shaft?

Teacher: It makes A-flat minor, of course.

In Ancient Egypt, what music did the mummies like most?

WRaP MuSic

Pupil: Mr. Lee, why do you suddenly have such a high singing voice?

Mr. Lee: I can't help it, it's my falsetto teeth.

Drums teacher: Why did you say you envy me?

Science teacher: Because you're allowed to tell your pupils to "beat it"!

Pupil: What music did people listen to when they built Stonehenge, sir?

Teacher: Heavy rock, I'd imagine!

Pupil: Why are opera singers afraid of cruise ships?

Teacher: Because they don't like the high Cs.

Teacher: Laura, how can you tell when your violin is out of tune?

Laura: It's easy. I just move the bow across the strings.

Teacher: Why are you all cheering?

Class: We just realized that the piano's locked.

Teacher: Then I'll sing until I find the right key!

Teacher: Anyone here any good at picking up music?

Nicky: Me, me, me!

Teacher: Great! Move that piano.

Completely mental arithmetic

Ali, if eggs cost 50 pence for 12, how many would you get for 25 pence?

None, I'd buy a bag of chips.

How many seconds are there in a year?

12. Second of January, second of February…

Clara, if I bought 100 buns for 50 cents, what would each bun be?

Stale.

Alfie, can you find the square root of nine?

Wow! Hasn't anyone else found it yet?

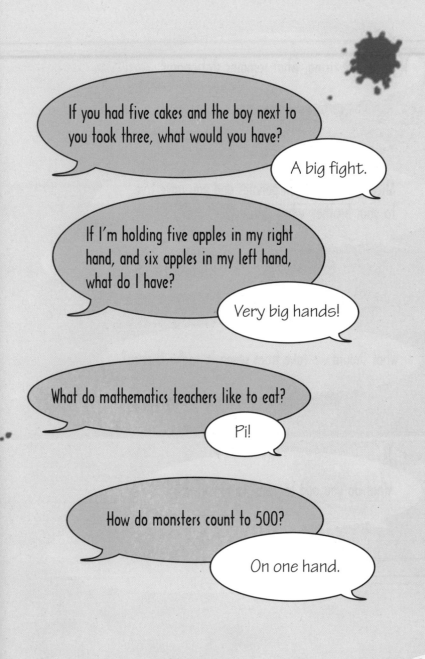

If you had five cakes and the boy next to you took three, what would you have?

A big fight.

If I'm holding five apples in my right hand, and six apples in my left hand, what do I have?

Very big hands!

What do mathematics teachers like to eat?

Pi!

How do monsters count to 500?

On one hand.

If prices are rising, what remains stationary?

Paper.

Alice, if you had ten pennies and you gave five to your brother, what would you have?

Ten pennies. I don't have a brother.

What should we take from seven to make it even?

The "s".

What do you add to zero, to make eight?

A tight belt, around its waist.

If you have 5,000 yen in one pocket, and 5,000 yen in another pocket, what would you have?

I'd have the wrong clothes on, Miss Smith.

What comes before eight?

My school bus, usually.

Really! A child of two could solve this problem!

Well, that's the problem… I'm ten.

The square of x plus the square of y equals the square of z. Got that?

No. Sorry sir, but nothing mathematics teachers say to me ever adds up.

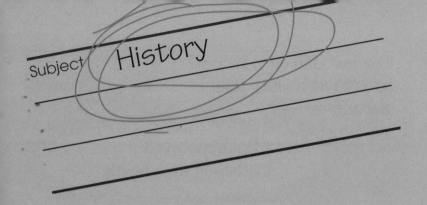
Teacher: Why do you wish you lived 200 years ago, Michael?

Michael: We wouldn't have so much history to learn, would we?

Teacher: Joseph, how long did Isaac Newton live?

Joseph: All his life, Mrs. Harris.

Teacher: Karen, when did Julius Caesar die?

Karen: A few days before his funeral?

Teacher: Why did you say that Rome was built at night?

Pupil: Because my dad told me that it wasn't built in a day.

Teacher: When I was at school, the subject I liked best was history.

Pupil: Excuse me, sir, wasn't it called current affairs in those days?

Teacher: How did ancient warriors learn their skills?

Pupil: At knight school!

Teacher: Frankie, do you know why George Washington was buried at Mount Vernon?

Frankie: Because he was dead, I reckon.

Name something important that didn't exist 100 years ago.

The modern world, miss.

Class wildlife

Teacher: If a flea was as big as a man, it could jump higher than a house. Why are you laughing, Don?

Don: Sir, houses can't jump!

Teacher: Can anybody tell me how animals in Africa know when it is time to migrate?

Pupil: Is it because they keep an eye on the gnus, sir?

Teacher: In this box, I have a ten foot snake. Why are you all laughing?

Class: Because snakes don't have feet, sir.

Meanwhile, in I.T. class...

How can you tell when a teacher's been using a computer?

There's correction fluid all over the screen.

Why is the I.T. teacher so tired?

Because she took a hard drive to work.

What food do I.T. teachers like most?

Chips.

What's the best way to break a computer?

Let a grown up use it.

There was an old teacher named Green,
Who invented a caning machine,
On the ninety-ninth stroke
The rotten thing broke
And made that cruel man a has-been.

Danny, where is your homework?
This is _not_ an essay.
Please _see me_!

You're in Trouble

You're in trouble

Every time I turn around, I catch you doing something you're not supposed to do. What can we do about that, Sally?

Tell me when you're about to turn around.

Sir, would you punish me for something I didn't do?

Of course not.

Good, because I didn't do my homework.

Are you chewing gum?

No, I'm Sarah Smith.

Johnnie, you know you can't sleep in my class.

You're right. But maybe if you were a little quieter I could.

Didn't you promise to behave today?

Yes, I did.

And didn't I promise to punish you if you didn't?

Yes, that's true. But since I broke my promise I don't mind if you break yours too.

You are the number one troublemaker in this class.

I always knew I'd be good at something.

Joey, why did you kick the computer?

Because you told me to boot it up.

Alex, this letter from your dad... it looks as if it's been written by you.

That's because he, um, borrowed my pen.

Why can't you ever answer my questions?

Well, if I could there wouldn't be much point in me being here, would there?

Where's your homework on gravity?

I dropped it.

Where's your homework on memory?

I forgot it.

Why haven't you brought in your homework on garbage disposal?

Because it was rubbish.

Why didn't you come to school yesterday?

Because I turned into a leopard.

That's ridiculous.

But I was covered in spots!

Why haven't you been to school for a month?

Well, I keep thinking I'm a snail. So by the time I've crawled to school, it's time to crawl home again.

Oh dear, I don't feel well.

Where don't you feel well?

Here, at school.

Who gave you that black eye?

No one gave it to me, I had to fight for it.

You missed school yesterday, didn't you?

Not a bit!

Sam! Are you copying Adam's answers?

No sir, I'm just checking to see if he's got his right.

Edward, go and stand outside the head teacher's study!

What for?

The rest of the lesson.

This is the third time I've had to speak to you this week. What do you have to say about that?

I say thank goodness it's Friday, Miss Smith.

Parent-teacher night

Teacher: With grades like these, there's only one thing I can say about your daughter, Mr. Brown.

Mr. Brown: What's that?

Teacher: She can't be cheating.

Parent: I'm outraged! I want to take my daughter out of this terrible mathematics class.

Teacher: But she came top.

Parent: Exactly!

Teacher: Mrs. Frost, last year you were worried that your son was going to fail.

Mrs. Frost: Yes, I remember.

Teacher: Well, your worries are over.

Teacher: Congratulations, Mrs. Clark. Your son has finally moved up from kindergarten. How does he feel?

Mrs. Clark: He's delighted. In fact, he was so excited he cut himself shaving.

Teacher: Your daughter is a wonder child, Mr. Day.

Mr. Day: Oh, that is good to know.

Teacher: Yes, I wonder if she ever listens to a thing I say.

Teacher: Your daughter's writing has improved 100% this year, Mrs. Lowe.

Mrs. Lowe: Excellent. I'm so pleased.

Teacher: The only problem is... now I can see all the spelling mistakes.

Teacher: Frank Smith is the stupidest boy in the class.

Mr. Smith: Oi! That's my son you're talking about!

Teacher: Oh, I'm sorry!

Mr. Smith: So am I. I have to live with him.

You're late

Why are you late, Stan?

I was on time until I saw a sign that said "SCHOOL AHEAD, SLOW DOWN".

You're late again!

I know. I even got a potato clock, like you suggested, but it was no help.

What? I simply told you to get up at eight o'clock, or earlier.

Oops! Maybe I should get my ears tested, too!

Amy, you should have been here at nine o'clock.

Why, what happened?

You're late!

I overslept.

What! You sleep at home, too?

Why are you crawling into school ten minutes late?

Well, you told me never to walk in late again.

Sorry I'm late sir. I was dreaming about soccer.

Why did that make you late?

They played overtime.

An old physics teacher named Bright,
Once managed to go faster than light,
He started one day
In the relative way
And returned on the previous night.

Charles Applethwait

What's your name?

Roll call

Teacher: What is your name?

Pupil: Al, sir.

Teacher: Al who?

Pupil: Al be asleep by the end of the roll call.

Teacher: King, Joseph.

Pupil: Here, sir.

Teacher: Hey, you must be "joking"! Ha-ha!

Pupil: Very funny, Mr. Cook.

Teacher: Name?

Pupil: Albie.

Teacher: Albie who?

Pupil: Albie blowed, you forgot my name.

Teacher: What is your name?

Pupil: Ariel.

Teacher: Ariel pain in the neck?

Pupil: No, Ariel joy to teach, that's me!

trouble

Teacher: Name?

Pupil: Liz.

Teacher: Liz who?

Pupil: Liz-en more carefully, I told you my name yesterday.

Teacher: What's your name?

Pupil: Karen, sir.

Teacher: Karen who?

Pupil: Karen you recognize me?

Teacher: And what's your name?

Pupil: Sarah.

Teacher: Sarah who?

Pupil: Sarah easy way to pass today's test?

Teacher: Name?

Pupil: Don Juan.

Teacher: Don Juan who?

Pupil: Don Juan to be in zees school today.

Teacher: Your name, please.

Pupil: Don.

Teacher: Don who?

Pupil: Don you know my name yet?

Teacher: Your name?

Pupil: Edward.

Teacher: Edward who?

Pupil: Edward be nice if you let us go home early today.

Teacher: Name?

Pupil: Dawn.

Teacher: Dawn who?

Pupil: Dawn you get sick of doing roll call, day in and day out?

Teacher: Name?

Pupil: Harry.

Teacher: Harry who?

Pupil: Harry up and get on with the lesson, sir!

Teacher: Name?

Pupil: Wendy.

Teacher: Wendy who?

Pupil: Wendy teacher's back
is turned, we all make faces.

Teacher: Name?

Pupil: Alfie.

Teacher: Alfie who?

Pupil: Oh not again... Alfie give your
forgetfulness, I know you're getting old.

The head teacher's office

Head teacher: So, you've been causing trouble. What's your name?

Pupil: Danielle.

Head teacher: Danielle who?

Pupil: Danielle at me, I've done nothing wrong.

Head teacher: So, you've been giving silly excuses to your teacher! What's your name?

Pupil: Alma.

Head teacher: Alma who?

Pupil: Alma homework got eaten by the dog, honestly.

Head teacher: I want you to tell me who broke the window. First, tell me your name.

Pupil: Doris.

Head teacher: Doris who?

Pupil: Doris no way I'm telling you anything.

Head teacher: Hmm, it appears I punished you by mistake last week. What's your name again?

Pupil: Aaron.

Head teacher: Aaron who?

Pupil: Aaron you going to say sorry to me?

Head teacher: Who are you?

Pupil: Noah, sir.

Head teacher: Noah who?

Pupil: Noah good joke, sir? I could do with a laugh!

Head teacher: The teacher sent you to see me because you didn't do your homework. What's your name?

Pupil: Alex.

Head teacher: Alex who?

Pupil: Alex-plain later. Can I go now?

Head teacher: And what is your name?

Pupil: Hutch.

Head teacher: Really? Hutch who?

Pupil: Bless you, sir.

Head teacher: You look upset. What's your name?

Pupil: Celeste.

Head teacher: Celeste who?

Pupil: Celeste time I saw a face like yours, I cried. Boo-hoo!

Head teacher: Name, boy.

Pupil: Frank Lee.

Head teacher: Frank Lee who?

Pupil: Frank Lee it's none of your business.

Head teacher: Who are you?
You act like you own the place.

Pupil: Alex.

Head teacher: Alex who?

Pupil: Look, Alex the
questions around here. Got that?

Head teacher: So, the terrible twins from Mr Lee's class have been sent to me. Now, remind me of your names.

Twins: Harv and Hugh.

Head teacher: Harv and Hugh who?

Twins: Harv and Hugh got better things to do
than ask us silly questions?

Head teacher: For the last time, I demand you tell me your name. There'll be trouble if you don't.

Pupil: Sadie.

Head teacher: Sadie who?

Pupil: Sadie magic word and then
I'll tell you.

A knock at the staffroom door

Knock knock!
Teacher: Who's there?
Pupil: Howell.
Teacher: Howell who?
Pupil: Howell you find out if you don't open the door?

Knock knock!
Teacher: Who's there?
Pupil: Hugo.
Teacher: Hugo who?
Pupil: Hugoing to let me in or what?

Knock knock!
Teacher: Who's there?
Pupil: Carrie.
Teacher: Carrie who?
Pupil: Carrie me up to see the nurse, I've hurt my leg.

Knock knock!

Teacher: Who's there?

Pupil: Ivan.

Teacher: Ivan who?

Pupil: Ivan to go home, please.

Knock knock!

Teacher: Who's there?

Pupil: Eileen.

Teacher: Eileen who?

Pupil: Eileen on your car and, guess what, it dents. Oops!

Knock knock!

Teacher: Who's there?

Pupil 1: Oscar...

Pupil 2: ...and Greta.

Teacher: Oscar and Greta who?

Pupil 1: Oscar stupid question...

Pupil 2: ...and Greta silly answer.

A right-handed teacher named Wright,
Wrote "rite" when she meant to write "right".
If she'd written right well
She'd have shown she could spell
And not written rot writing right.

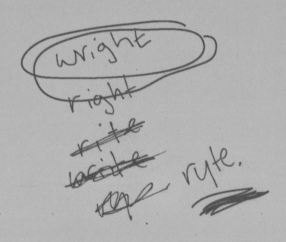

Not so smart

Teacher: James, you've been cheating.

James: How did you know?

Teacher: Well, where Bill's answer says "I don't know!" you put "Me neither!"

Teacher: Kevin, your ideas are like flawless diamonds.

Kevin: Thank you sir. Is that because they are so brilliant and valuable?

Teacher: No, it's because they are so rare.

Pupil: Mr. Lee, does ham grow on trees?

Mr. Lee: Of course not.

Pupil: Well, what's an ambush then?

Teacher: Jane, how did you manage to get all those splinters in your hand?

Jane: I don't know, miss. I just scratched my head.

Pupil: When I grow up I'm going to be a cop and follow in my father's footsteps.

Teacher: I'm glad to hear that, but I didn't know your dad was a police officer.

Pupil: He's not, he's a burglar.

Teacher: How do dolphins stay in touch?

Pupil: They send sea mails to each other!

Teacher: What's that you're reading, Edward?

Edward: Don't know, sir.

Teacher: But you're reading out loud.

Edward: Yeah, but I'm not listening.

Teacher: Karen, what on earth are you doing standing on your head?

Karen: Well you just told us to turn things over in our minds.

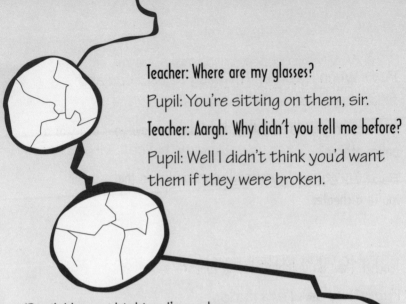

Teacher: Where are my glasses?

Pupil: You're sitting on them, sir.

Teacher: Aargh. Why didn't you tell me before?

Pupil: Well I didn't think you'd want them if they were broken.

Pupil: I keep thinking I'm a dog.

Teacher: Oh, don't be so ridiculous. Now go back to your desk and sit down.

Pupil: I can't, sir. I'm not allowed on the furniture.

Pupil: Is it true that the number nine no longer exists?

Teacher: Of course not. What made you think that?

Pupil: Well, I'm sure I heard you say "seven ate nine".

Teacher: Danielle, you never get anything right. What on earth are you going to do when you leave school?

Danielle: I thought I'd become a TV weather girl. They never get anything right, either.

Pupil: Why *do* you keep calling me squirrel, sir?

Teacher: Because you drive me nuts.

Pupil: Why *do* you keep calling me big cat, Mrs. Harris?

Mrs. Harris: Because I've come to the conclusion that you're a cheater.

Pupil: Mr. Cook, is the English Royal Family stupid?

Mr. Cook: Certainly not! Why do you ask?

Pupil: Well why did they build Windsor Castle so close to Heathrow airport?

Silly teachers

How old do you think the history teacher is?

At least 40. Because my brother's 20 and the history teacher is twice as annoying as my brother.

Ask the teacher what worms taste like.

Why? How will she know?

Because there was one in the apple that I just gave her.

What's the difference between a dull teacher and a dull book?

You can shut the book up!

Why does that teacher wear dark glasses?

Because he likes to keep his pupils in the dark.

Did you hear that our nutty science teacher has taken down his front doorbell?

Yeah. He's obsessed with winning the no-bell prize.

Why did you just call the dullest teacher in the school "absolutely fascinating"?

Because he's standing behind you, right now!

How many jokes about silly teachers are there?

None! They're all true.

Don't say this about teacher

She's an experiment in Artifical Stupidity.

He's a few clowns short of a circus.

He's a few straws shy of a bale.

She's a few yards short of the hole.

The wheel's spinning, but the hamster's dead.

Her receiver's off the hook.

He's all wax and no wick.

She's a few sandwiches short of a picnic.

She has enough straw in her head to bed an elephant.

He has his brain on cruise control.

She's having a party in her head, but nobody's invited.

She's a few beans short of a casserole.

If his brains were taxed, he'd get a rebate.

If his brains were dynamite, we'd have nothing to worry about.

If you stand close enough to his head, you can hear the sea.

He's out to lunch and won't be back.

She's a few feathers short of the whole duck.

She has a defective hard drive.

He couldn't organize a food fight at a birthday party.

The lights are on, but nobody's home.

His elevator doesn't go all the way to the top.

He has a few buttons missing on his remote control.

Her mouth's in gear, but her brain's in neutral.

She has an IQ lower than a snake's belly in a ditch.

He forgot to pay his brain bill.

He's one bit short of a byte.

If he had another brain, it'd be lonely.

He's a bit slow out of the gate.

She's not as smart as the average bear.

A peculiar teacher named Ray,
Used to teach in a very odd way,
He gave lessons in verse
But it made matters worse
So the moral is: rhyme just don't pay!

school food and sickness

Lunchtime

Pupil: Yuck! There's a fly in my soup.
Cook: Shush, you'll make the other kids jealous.

Pupil: Oh no, what's this fly doing in my soup?
Cook: Looks like it's drowning, to me.

Pupil: Oh no! I've got a fly in my soup, too!
Cook: You're mistaken. That's a cockroach.

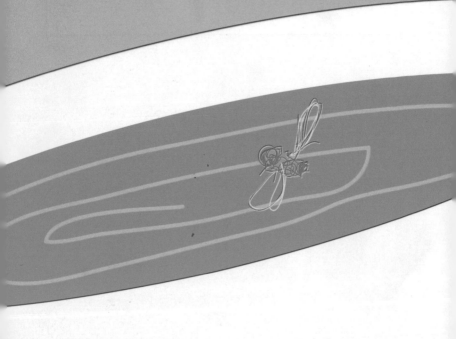

Jim: What has eyes but can't see?

Jane: A school cafeteria potato.

Tom: What do school cheese and our school cook's nose have in common?

Tim: They both smell, and they're both runny.

Teacher: Clara, if you take a pie from the school cafeteria and eat three-quarters, what are you left with?

Clara: Stomach ache.

Pupil: Sir, this meal's half cold!

Teacher: Well eat the other half then.

Pupil: Sir, you just sat on some grapes.

Teacher: Ah, I thought I just heard something let out a little wine.

Teacher: Why did you say that school cooks are even crueller than teachers?

Pupil: Because they batter fish, beat eggs and whip cream.

Charlie: I wonder why school meat is so tough.

Mike: I'm not sure, but I heard the cook say that it was full of iron.

Teacher: You've got your finger in my soup!

Pupil: It's okay, it isn't hot.

Pupil: What's the difference between school dinners and fresh horse droppings?

Teacher: Not much, except that one is fresher and warmer than the other.

Zoë: Why do you think the school soccer team make such a mess when they eat?

Chloë: Because they all like to dribble.

Pupil: This food must be really clean, you know.

Teacher: Why's that?

Pupil: Because it tastes of soap!

Pupil: What kind of pie is this? It tastes like glue.

Cook: That would be the apple pie. The plum pie tastes like paint.

New girl: Why is the school nurse's office next to the school cafeteria?

New girl's friend: Taste the food, then you'll find out.

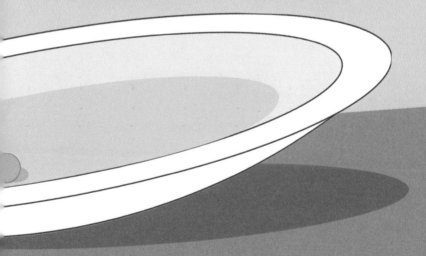

Pupil: These peas are as hard as bullets.

Teacher: Let me taste them.... Hmm, they seem soft enough to me!

Pupil: Well they would, I've been chewing them for the last half an hour.

Problems, problems

Pupil: Help, I need to see the nurse, I've only got 60 seconds to live.

Teacher: Just wait a minute, please, Johnny.

Teacher: Good grief, Wendy, what are you taking for that cough?

Wendy: How much will you give me for it, sir?

Pupil: Please miss, I have a problem. Could you help me out?

Teacher: Yes, I'll hold the door for you.

Pupil: Can I go and see the nurse, please? I think I'm turning into a waste bin.

Teacher: Don't talk rubbish.

Pupil: Miss Smith, I'm so tired but I can't sleep. What should I do?

Miss Smith: Lie on the edge of your bed, and you'll soon drop off.

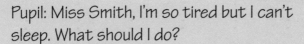

Please can I go and see the nurse? I think I've turned invisible.

I'm sorry, I don't think she'll be able to see you just now.

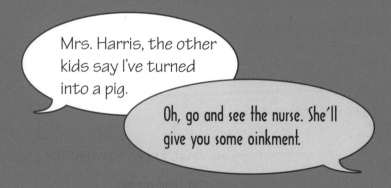

Mrs. Harris, the other kids say I've turned into a pig.

Oh, go and see the nurse. She'll give you some oinkment.

Pupil: Help me, Mr. Jones. I've just swallowed a roll of film.

Mr. Jones: Just go and sit in a darkened room. We'll wait and see what develops.

Help, I've lost my memory.

When did this happen?

When did what happen?

Pupil: Please miss, there's something wrong with me. I can see into the future.

Teacher: That's amazing. When did this start?

Pupil: Next Thursday.

Pupil: Oh Mr. Lee. I've cut myself really badly.

Mr. Lee: Well, just listen to this joke, it'll have you in stitches.

Pupil: Miss, I keep thinking that there's two of me.

Teacher: For goodness sake, one at a time please.

Restaurant

Pupil: Teacher, teacher, I keep getting lost. I can never find the right room for my classes.

Waiter: You do have a problem, young lady. This is a restaurant.

Pupil: Mr. Cook, I keep thinking I'm a little birdie.

Mr. Cook: Go and see the nurse right away. She'll give you some tweatment.

Pupil: Mr. Lee. I think I'm shrinking.

Mr. Lee: Well, go and wait at the nurse's office, and be a little patient.

Teacher: My, you look tired Joey.

Joey: Oh, the problem is that I snore so loudly I wake myself up.

Teacher: Well, sleep in another room then.

Miss Smith, I feel like a deck of cards.

Go and sit down, I'll deal with you later. And for goodness sake, stop shuffling.

Pupil: Mr. Lee, I feel like a car.
Can I go and see the nurse?

Mr. Lee: Yes, you do look tired, and exhausted.

Why am I covered in wheel marks, Miss Smith?

Well, it looks to me as if you've allowed yourself to get run down.

Pupil: Oh Mr. Cook, I don't feel well. My nose keeps running and my feet smell.

Mr. Cook: Hmm. You'd better go and see the nurse. It looks to me as if life has turned you upside down.

Sir, I think your face looks like a clock.

You're just trying to wind me up.

In the old days a teacher named Bind,
Gave my dad, in a manner unkind,
Heavy whacks to the head
With a flat piece of lead
Saying "This lesson will broaden your mind!"

school's
out

Teacher's car

A teacher walks into a service station and asks the mechanic:

Could you get a headlight for my car?

The mechanic walks around the car, scratches his head, thinks a little, and then says:

I'm not sure that's a fair trade, you know...

How does a teacher double the value of his car?

He fills the tank up.

A teacher is driving along a country road. He comes across a donkey. The donkey, never having seen such a decrepit vehicle, says, "My goodness, what are you?" The teacher's car replies, "Why, I'm a car, of course." The donkey says, "Yeah right. And I'm a horse."

What happened to the carpentry teacher's car?

Wooden start!

What did the teacher say when his car got to the top of the hill?

It's a miracle!

Which teacher never gets his hair wet in the shower?

A bald one.

Why did the teacher put sugar under his pillow?

He needed to make his dreams sweeter!

What meals do mathematics teachers like most?

Take aways!

Why did the art teacher take a sketch pad to bed with her?

So that she could draw the curtains.

Look who's talking!

A teacher walks into a shop with a pig under his arm...

A shop assistant walks over.

My, that's the ugliest animal I've ever seen. Where on earth did you get it?

I won him in a raffle.

Home time

Pupil: Dad, I saved some money today. I resisted the temptation to catch the bus and walked home instead.

Pupil's dad: Why didn't you resist the temptation to catch a taxi? You'd have saved more.

My teacher was doing bird impressions today.

Oh really, how nice. What did she do?

She watched me like a hawk.

Pupil: Today, my teacher asked me if I have any younger brothers or sisters who will be coming to my school.

Pupil's mother: That's nice of her, dear. But did you tell her that you are an only child?

Pupil: Yes. She said, "Thank goodness!"

Pupil's dad: What did you learn at school today, son?

Pupil: I learned that the homework you did for me was all wrong!

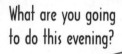

What are you going to do this evening?

I'm going to help my dad with my homework.

Pupil: Oh dear, I had a terrible day at school. The other girls all said I have big feet.

Pupil's mother: That's nonsense.

Pupil: And there's a school skiing trip, but you said last year that we couldn't afford skis.

Pupil's mother: That's no problem, I'm sure you'll just be able to use your shoes.

End of term report

Look at this report! You were behind all your classmates again!

That's nonsense, Dad! I sat at the front all through the year.

Look at this report! Your teacher says she can't teach you anything!

I told you she was useless.

Oh dear. Everything is going up. Food prices, fuel prices, clothes prices. Why can't anything go down?

Here Mum, take a look at my grades!

How were your exam results this year, son?

Underwater, Dad! They were all below C level.

93

Teacher's worst jokes

How was the naughty train punished?

It had to write railway lines.

Why did the toad visit the mushroom?

He thought it was a toad-school.

Which English king was good at fractions?

Henry the Eighth

What disease do art teachers get?

Pencilitis

Has anyone ever seen the Abominable Snowman?

Not yeti.

Name another flower in the chrysanthemum family.

Chrysanthe-dad

Name two animals that live in India.

A tiger and his sister.

Where do you find edible beetles?

Depends where you left them.

What do you get if you cross the school bell with an alarm clock?

Something that wakes you up when it's time to go home.

First published in 2003 by Usborne Publishing Ltd,
Usborne House, 83-85 Saffron Hill, London, EC1N 8RT, England.
www.usborne.com

Printed in Italy.